A BU… IES

Daisy Neal

To: Merry and Bob.

"The Lord is good, a strong hold in the day of trouble; and He knoweth them that trust in Him." Nahum. 1. v7.

With love from,

Auntie Daisy.

9th January. 1995.

ARTHUR H. STOCKWELL LTD.
Elms Court Ilfracombe Devon
Established 1898

First published in Great Britain, 1995

By the same author:
Poems of Praise and Promise
Pearls Within
Sing and Soar
A Ring of Rubies

Dedicated to my two young friends
Tim and Sue Hoyle,
praying the Lord will encourage them
as they have encouraged me.

ISBN 0 7223 2858-3

*Printed in Great Britain by
Arthur H. Stockwell Ltd.
Elms Court Ilfracombe
Devon*

CONTENTS

YOUR COMPUTER

Make the most of your computer. Store in it everything possible, for you never know when what is stored will come in useful.

I wish I had stored more in mine.

But do I hear you say, "I do not have a computer." Oh! yes you have, and there is no maker of these instruments to compare with the One Who made yours. Have you guessed what I am writing about? Your brain, of course.

How I regret I did not store more in mine when I was young, for had I done so I could have written hundreds of stories similar to these in this little book; and I would have been much more appreciative of many things in life.

As you know, I was born in Stafford, but only now am I realising what a wonderful old town it is. In my youth I took little notice of a small portion remaining of the great wall which once surrounded the town; or of the Gaol and the Law Courts and many other old buildings. As far as I was concerned, they were just there and part of my everyday life. I know differently now.

And why did I not take in more of what older people could tell me? How I wish now that I had done so. My parents had a very old friend who had heard Spurgeon preach, and he said, "When Spurgeon preached, people trembled in their seats." That was one thing I do remember because it appealed to my imagination. Oh! for preachers like him today, for if there were, I believe there would be less lawlessness in our nation and fewer dreadful crimes.

My mother came from the Birmingham area, and she told me of a man and his wife who often came to the Bull Ring. The lady had a most beautiful voice, and would sing, accompanied by her husband on a little organ. Mother said the crowd soon gathered when they heard this lovely voice, and she liked, best of all to hear her sing, "Somebody came and lifted me. Out of my sin and misery. Who could it be, Oh! who could it be, Who could it be, but Jesus?" How I should love to have heard this lady sing, and see the rapt attention of the crowd as they listened.

So, if you are a mother or father reading this little book, impress upon your children the benefits of storing their computers while they are young with good and useful and interesting items.

"Whatsoever things are true, whatsoever things are honest, whatsoever things are just, whatsoever things are pure, whatsoever things are lovely, whatsoever things are of good report . . . . think on these things." *Philippians 4 8.*

"Somebody holds my hand each day,
Guiding my feet lest I should stray,
Walking with Him, how blessed the way!
Who can it be but Jesus?"

"Who could it be, Oh! who could it be,
Who could it be, but Jesus?
Who could it be, Oh! who could it be,
Who could it be, but Jesus?"

Fred P. Morris

A GRACIOUS LADY

A few miles from Stafford there is a lovely little village, and in the centre of it a row of Railway Cottages. In one of them lived a retired signalman and his wife whom we often visited. This man was of the type usually termed 'A real character'. His eyes were blue and always twinkling with merriment. He was tall, about six feet four, thin and stooped a little. He had large feet which were quite a problem when it came to playing the American organ in the village chapel, for large feet do not very well fit into the small pedal space.

I first met him when he came to our family home to invite me to sing at the village chapel. At the ring of the door bell one of my sisters answered it, and there stood Sam looking down at her. "Does Miss Daisy Fletcher live here?" he asked. My sister assented. "Can I see her?" he asked. "Tell her a 'little man' would like to see her." My sister duly delivered the message and I thought she had rather an amused look on her face. You can imagine my surprise when I found myself looking up into the twinkling blue eyes of this very tall man. And this was the beginning of a very happy friendship between Sam and his wife and myself, and later with my husband too.

But the incident I most clearly remember concerning Sam took place in his own home. My husband and I were visiting them; Mrs B was alone when we arrived but Sam soon came in. "I've been to Stafford today" he announced. And here I would explain that, having been employed by the Railway, he travelled many miles, visiting friends, always taking with him a packet of sandwiches and requesting nothing more than a cup of tea to drink with them, indeed he would never accept anything more. So, "I've been to Stafford today, and I was just going to go up the Library steps when I see the Countess of Shrewsbury coming down, so I waited for her and I said, 'You are the Countess of Shrewsbury aren't you?' 'Yes' she says. 'Well, I'm Sam B — from Hayward and they call me the *General Factotum* of the village'; so she puts out her hand and says, 'Well, I am very pleased to meet you, Mr B —'."

Now Sam's wife was a very prim and proper lady, and with a look of horror she said, "You didn't say that Sam?" "Of course I did" he replied. "And why not? And she didn't mind."

As I listened to Sam tell this story and then looked at us with great amusement at his wife's reaction, I thought 'What a gracious lady, the Countess of Shrewsbury,' and she was the wife of the Senior Earl of England.

Perhaps, dear reader, you are growing older, and you love the Lord and want to serve Him, but there is now so little you can do. Remember you can always be gracious. I find in these days that people are so busy few have time to spare even to say a few words of greeting. How encouraging are just a few words, graciously spoken, accompanied by a kindly smile. Such a brief pause can mean so much, and there are many, many people so badly in need of a gracious encounter with someone.

Do you remember the hymn which says,

"Gracious Spirit, dwell with me;
I myself would gracious be;
And with words that help and heal
Would Thy life in mine reveal.
And with actions bold and meek
Would for Christ my Saviour speak."

THE FAMILY BOND

We lived in Stafford and my husband had preaching appointments on the Methodist Local Preachers' Plan of the Stafford Circuit. Together we cycled many miles to little country chapels where he was appointed to preach, sometimes for one service, at others for morning and evening services. We loved cycling through the beautiful Staffordshire countryside, along minor roads and little country lanes.

Sometimes he was booked for only one service, but at other times for both morning and evening services, when we were given hospitality for the day. In one lovely village it was usual for him to take two services, and we spent the day always with the same family, and we became great friends and loved them very dearly, Father, Mother, three children – two girls and a boy, and a dear old Gran. After the evening service we returned to the home, joined by other friends from the Chapel, and with Dad playing the violin, and someone at the organ, we joined in singing the great old hymns of our Faith. How sweet the memories of those times are to me now!

For a number of years we greatly enjoyed this happy fellowship until, to our great sorrow, a man of Communist persuasion came to live in the village and insidiously captured our friend's mind with his teaching, and after awhile he ceased to attend Chapel, and gradually the family followed suit, but dear old Gran continued to go alone as long as she was able. In spite of our friend's changed views, he still insisted we go to his home when we came to the Chapel; but the atmosphere was changed. Dear Gran sat in her corner by the fireplace and told us they laughed at her for reading her Bible and the *Christian Herald*. We were so sorry for her.

Then we went abroad, but always called to see our friends when we were on leave. Gran said the situation for her in the home was worsening, and we did our best to encourage her. But calling to see them during one leave we were told Gran was very ill, unconscious and not expected to live long. Two or three of the 'new friends' were at the home. We asked if we might see Gran, but her niece said there would be no point in our going to see her as she would not know us, and one of the visitors said, "She would not know you for she does not know us." But we insisted on seeing her, and followed her niece upstairs.

Our friends' house was a beautiful, old timbered building and we went up the steep oak stairs, into Gran's room where she was lying on her bed between pure white sheets, and the black timbered beams of the ceiling above her.

I sat on a chair beside her bed, my husband stood beside me while Gran's niece leaned on the railings at the bottom of the bed. I took Gran's hand and said quietly, "How are you, Gran?" Slowly she opened her eyes, looked at us for a few seconds and then said, "Mr and Mrs Neal! When did you come home?" We told her. She then lifted one arm and pointing upwards said, "I'm going to my Heavenly Home. I'm going to my Heavenly Home. Pray for me Mr Neal." Her niece burst into a flood of tears and rushed from the room. My husband prayed, we both gave her a kiss and went downstairs. She went to her Heavenly Home very shortly after our visit.

Never before, nor have I since that episode experienced so strongly and so surely the mystic bond there is between members of the Lord's family. And I have often wondered what the 'new' friends said when Gran's niece went sobbing downstairs to them. They had left when we went down and we went straight home.

As Charles Wesley says, "All praise to our redeeming Lord, Who joins us by His grace" — and He does join us, by invisible bonds. Finishing the hymn Wesley says, "And if our fellowship below with Jesus be so sweet. What heights of rapture shall we know, When round His throne we meet."

I am longing to meet dear old Gran again.

A BOY AND A BIRD

The flats where I live are built on either side of a small courtyard. The main block is opposite my smaller block, and is alongside a busy road. Entrance to the courtyard is under a wide archway, for there is a flat on the archway itself.

From my windows I have an excellent view of the comings and goings of both people and cars, and as there are not many flats, I know all the residents and a stranger is soon spotted.

One afternoon I saw a schoolboy of about fifteen coming through the archway, holding his hands in front of him, cupped together, obviously carrying something carefully. Reaching a row of low shrubs, he stooped down, opened his hands and a baby starling hopped out, and after standing a second or two disappeared into the bushes. The boy then went away.

I wondered, 'Where had that little bird come from to be picked up from the pavement outside?' 'How kind of that boy,' I thought. But what could the little thing do without the mother; it could not fly.

Having a great love for birds, I tried to keep my eye on the situation as much as possible. For some time nothing happened, then a little head peeped out from between the shrub leaves; a quick look round and back it went. Another peep around and then the little thing emerged enough for me to see him. At this stage he must have cheeped, for a starling flew swiftly across from the right side of the courtyard and immediately began to feed the little one. Several times she did this and I thought of Elijah on his long journey fleeing from Jezebel; tired and weary he fell asleep, and was awakened by an angel to find a cake baked and a cruse of water, and the angel said, "Arise and eat, for the journey is too great for thee." So this mother starling fed her little one before beginning to lure it from beneath the shrubs. This she did by enticing it out a little then flying off to a garden of a house which is beside the flats. Then she came back to it and the little one hopped along a little further, and so the flights backwards and forwards by the mother continued, and the little bird followed her call bit by bit, until it disappeared round the corner of my little block where there is a strip of garden. But the end of the story I do not know!

But it was all so lovely to me. How tenderly that boy carried that tiny bird and placed it by the shrubs! How that little bird's instinct led it to shelter there and be still! How the mother found the baby! How she first fed it before enticing it to leave a shelter! How she flew backwards and forwards and gradually led it on to safety.

I thought what a picture it was of our Heavenly Father's patience and tenderness towards His children.

The boy from Warwick School had no idea that his kind action was observed but I think how lovely it would be if this book could come into his hands and he could read how touched I was by his kindly care for a little bird of whom some would say, "It is only a starling!"

"Like as a father pitieth His children, so the Lord pitieth them that fear Him." *Psalm 103 13.*

"The Lord is good to all and His tender mercies are over all His works." *Psalm 145 9.*

SPOT ON TIME

In common with many retired people, my friends John and Ruth had realised that their garden was now too large for them to manage, and so began to look for another home with a smaller garden, not wishing to be without one. But where to find just what they wanted was their problem. The matter was committed to the Lord.

They looked around the Midlands, which they knew well; they looked in different areas of Devon, but found nothing suitable. At last, in North Wales they were led to a property which satisfied all their hopes — a small bungalow with a small garden.

I had prayed much for my friends, and was greatly concerned when I heard they were going to live where they did not know anyone. Having lived in a seaside resort for a number of years, I have seen terrible tragedies befall couples, who, on retirement have pulled up all their roots and gone to live where they think life will be wonderful for them, and then, suddenly and unexpectedly, one or the other has died, leaving behind a devastated, lonely partner.

John and Ruth arrived in their new home on the first Monday in April. On the Wednesday I received a monthly magazine I take, and glancing quickly through the 'letters' page, read one where a lady asked if any readers had a recipe for Elderberry Syrup. Having a lovely one, I typed out the recipe right away to send to her, and wrote a short letter to go with it. When I looked for the address, which was at the bottom of the letter, where should it be but Aber-- in North Wales where my friends had gone. I was amazed! So I decided to tell the lady of my friends' arrival there and that they knew no one. I said I had no idea of the size of the town, but wondered whether it would be possible for her to call in and see them. For all I knew the lady could be old and unable to get about.

Some days later, John rang me. A lady had called to see them with a letter in her hand, and giving them my name, asked them if they knew such a person. "Of course we know her," they said, and asked her in. Who was this lady? The wife of an Evangelical Minister, who with her husband

and three beautiful daughters, lived just round the corner from my friends. And what a sweet time of fellowship they had together.

Still more amazing is the fact that, writing to me after meeting John and Ruth, this dear lady told me it was a little over a year since she had written to the magazine asking about the recipe!

How perfectly the Lord times everything when we commit our cares and problems to Him. Before we call, He has the answer. And so John and Ruth have friends who will do all they can to help them, and for myself, I have friends to whom I can write, and for whom I can pray for the Lord's blessing on their work for Him.

There is no need to be perplexed,
Or with life's problems be distressed,
For the Lord has the answer NOW.
Before you called, He heard your cry
And He will every need supply,
In measure, exceedingly above
All that you ever asked or thought,
Because of His exceeding love
FOR YOU.

Daisy Neal

"Before they call, I will answer; and while they are yet speaking, I will hear." *Isaiah 65 24.*

HIS PLANS

Many of you will remember a song which was extremely popular at one time, which had a line repeated again and again, "I did it MY way". My reaction to it has always been, "What a mistake". Perhaps some of you who read this article will say, "Yes, I did it MY way once, and how I wish I had not."

I am sure most of us have seen someone trying to teach a child how to do something but the little one shakes the head and says "No, No."

Many young Christians, I believe, take such attitudes. They do not say to the Lord, "I'll do it my way," or "No, no," but they do go their own way by not consulting Him about every part of daily life. There was a time when I did not. Not deliberately but through ignorance.

When I was a teenager, I became friendly with a young man; we were both members of the same church. It is difficult for members of the opposite sex to become friends without the other church members anticipating romance! But I became very unhappy about the relationship. What could I do? Just at the time of my unhappy perplexity, a Methodist Pastor and his wife came to conduct a Mission in a village, and I was asked to go and sing at some of the services, and the Pastor and his wife preached on alternate evenings.

On the evening forever engraved upon my memory, Sister May preached. One sentence was emblazoned upon my heart — "So often we make our own plans, and ask God to bless them, but do we ever pray, 'Show me Thy plans for me'?"

I was struck by this, 'Show me Thy plans for me', and I thought 'Why, I have never asked the Lord to show me His plans for me.'

These words rang in my ears as I cycled home, and I began to pray, "Show me THY plans for me, Lord," and in but a few days the Lord gave me courage to break with the young man. And has the Lord not promised to "Do exceeding abundantly above all that we ask or think"? *Ephes. 3 20.* Indeed He has, and He fulfilled His promise to me, for in but a few weeks after asking Him daily to show me His plans for me, I met the man who became my husband. It was wonderful. My whole life was changed.

When the Lord called my husband a few years ago, we lived in the end house of a small row of what are termed 'Town-houses', which were situated in a walled garden where once stood a large old house. It was very lovely, very convenient, being right in the little town, but also very, very lonely. My birthday is in November and on the first one I spent alone, it poured with rain all day, and I saw no one at all. What did I do? You will easily guess. I prayed, "Lord, show me Thy plans for me," and He brought me to Warwick. But that is another story.

"Teach me Thy way, O Lord." *Psalm 86 11.*

THE OPERATION

Books are not written about their achievements, their faithful service does not make newspaper headlines, but day by day and year by year, they faithfully serve their Lord in obscurity, often in appalling conditions, their achievements unseen, often unknown but for a very few privileged people who have had the opportunity to see them at work. My husband and I were so favoured, not only in seeing them at work, but in hearing from them stories of how the Lord undertook for them in most difficult situations.

Who are these people to whom I refer? They are Salvation Army missionaries.

One Captain, a nurse, invited us to accompany her to do a weekly distribution of tablets to people suffering from leprosy. A special hut had been erected midway between a number of villages, where patients could go to receive their treatment. About fifty patients were gathered on the day of our visit. As many as possible crowded into the hut where a little table was erected at one end, and on it the Nurse arranged her papers and bottles of tablets with one or two other items. One by one the patients went up to the table and were scrutinized by the Nurse and then the required number of tablets handed to them which they had to swallow while she watched them; these were washed down by water drunk from little tin cans which the patients had to supply themselves. As I write I recapture the scene vividly of the Africans standing around in groups, in the dim light of the hut; and the Nurse in her white uniform at the table, and the patients throwing the tablets into their mouths, and then drinking water from discarded tin cans of all sizes.

The village where the Captain was stationed was very isolated, at the top of a steep escarpment, a few miles from our home. There the Salvation Army had a well-established Corps and Clinic. At one time a Norwegian couple were in charge, a Major and Mrs D---; the Major having charge of the Corps while his wife ran the clinic. Having been a Sister Tutor, she was a very skilful Nurse, and from her we heard the story of the operation.

Deep in the bush was a little village where one of the women was expecting a baby, and when the arrival of the child was imminent, a group of men arrived to escort Mrs D to the village, so she packed her bag and off she went with them, and it was not unusual for her to go in the middle of the night through the dark forest, protected by several men, to see a sick person or deliver a baby.

The woman was lying on the floor of the hut on a blanket, surrounded by a number of old women, whom Mrs D ushered outside in order to have room to do her work, and also that the patient might be kept quiet. But, unseen by her, one of them crept back, no doubt in order to watch the proceedings and report details to the other old cronies.

The baby arrived safely — a little girl — but to her dismay, Mrs D saw that she had five fingers and a thumb on both hands. The old woman saw this too and letting out a shriek, rushed outside to inform the waiting group. What a hullabuloo followed! Mrs D had to go outside and order them to be quiet or the mother would die from fright. Why all this dreadful wailing? Because children born with hands like this little one were said to possess an evil spirit.

Mrs D knew all this too, but what was she to do? If she left the child they would throw it into the bush to be eaten by wild animals. There was only one thing she could do, take the baby home with her and operate on the tiny hands as soon as possible. She knew that such an operation should not be done so soon, and yet it was a matter of life or death for this helpless little child.

She took her home. After a few days, the operation must be done, to delay was dangerous in case the child was stolen, and so this brave woman prepared to operate. When all was ready, she prayed, "Oh! God help me. Never have I needed Thy help so urgently; help me now," and then she set about the delicate operation on those tiny hands. The result was perfect.

And now tricky negotiations had to be undertaken to induce the mother to take her baby. A message was sent to the father to come and see the child. He came, but would only stand at the door and look at her, with a good space between them as Mrs D showed him the little hands, and he took in what he saw. He came again when it was suggested he brought the mother to see her baby. She did come but would not go near the child, but on a later visit was enticed inside to take a closer look. A few more visits and mother love prevailed and she took the little one in her arms. Later on she agreed to bath the child and at last, took her home. What a triumph for that dear Officer, and how she and her husband praised the Lord Who had given them the victory over the powers of evil.

When we saw the child she was about three years of age, a bright, happy active little girl, who looked with big, bright, wondering eyes at the two strange Abruni (white) man and woman looking at her.

But how different the story would have ended had Major and Mrs D not been at that particular Corps at that particular time.

What a remarkable story this is, which few will have heard, and how marvellously the Lord answered the prayer of His faithful servant.

"Call unto Me, and I will answer thee, and show thee great and mighty things which thou knowest not." *Jeremiah 33 3.*

RESCUED

"Youths watch woman drown." This was the astonishing caption of an article in a local newspaper.

About a couple of miles from my home there is a beautiful park, and through it runs a river, and on a beautiful June day a Peace Festival had been held there, attended by many people. Now evening was closing in and the crowd was dispersing.

A man from the town was talking to two New Age Travellers, when they noticed a gang of about forty youths just standing and gazing across the river. Looking for the reason for such rapt attention, they saw a woman, floating motionless under the water. The Traveller threw down his bum bag, and he and his friend dived into the river to rescue her. They gave her the kiss of life, but the youths ignored their pleas to lend them a warm article of clothing in which to wrap her until the ambulance arrived.

When the Traveller turned to pick up his bag which contained all his money — it had been stolen!

The local man said the youths were standing gazing at the drowning woman as though looking at a television picture. They told the Travellers they were "mad" to go into the river to save the woman.

But the man who had been talking with the Travellers took them home with him! What a contrast in loving kindness and wicked indifference.

How I thought of the Lord Jesus Christ as I read this story. I thought of all the people who watched Him die on the cross. Of the soldiers who gambled for His only possession — His seamless robe. And the two thieves dying on either side of Him, one who uttered abuse against Him, and the other who said, "Lord, remember me when Thou comest into Thy Kingdom" — *Luke 23 42* and the Lord's gracious reply, "Today shalt thou be with me in Paradise." Imagine it! When the Lord had completed His work of Redemption, He Himself took to Heaven with Him the first cleansed sinner — a thief. What a loving Saviour He is!

How I should love to know the thoughts of the woman whom the Travellers rescued from a watery grave.

May I ask you who read this article, "What do you think of the Lord Jesus Christ Who gave up all to save your soul from eternal death? Who suffered so much at the hands of sinners that you might become a child of God and have a home in Heaven?" Consider this and give your answer to the One Who died to save you.

He came
  the sinless Son of God,
  to rescue me.
How can it be that He
  Who knew no sin,
  should so love me?
That stripped of Heavenly glory
  a lot on earth He chose,
  living in poverty with those
Deep stained in sin.

And on the cross
  at Calvary,
From His hands
  and feet and side,
Flowed His sinless blood —
  a crimson tide,
To wash away in love
  the sin of those
  for whom He died.

Daisy Neal

VERSES FOR THE HELP AND INSPIRATION OF OLD CHRISTIAN 'FUDDY-DUDDIES'

"Old Christian Fuddy-duddies"
I heard the preacher say,
Puzzled, I thought, 'Why, who are they?'
Searching Concordance gave no clue
for a text in the Guide Book –
by daily use worn – the truth to pursue.
But what is this I clearly read?
* "In old age they shall still bear fruit?"
Why! surely this is most uncommon!
But God Who says it does not lie
Then how can I the truth deny?

Yet more the Guide Book has to tell
these poor old Christian 'Fuddy-duds'.
* As Lebanon's evergreen cedars,
Planted firm on banks of rivers,
drinking from the waters fresh
grow strong and tall above all trees,
So surely shall God's chosen be
Though tossed by many adverse winds,
Oft bent by weight of winter snows,
still firm and beautiful they stand
Securely held by God's strong hand.

The Guide Book more keenly I search,
this Book which is all about Christ;
I want to find what it has to explain
About all those called by His Name.
Why! daily blessings for you, old friend:
* God counts your steps, also your hairs,
* and to old age He has promised
to guard and guide you in life's cares.
And although your steps are slow
and white the hairs of your head,
* the beauty of the Lord your God
Shall be upon you, He has said.

These old 'Fuddy-duddies' in their youth
learned from the Guide Book a certain truth.
* As freely from the Lord you receive
Blessings abundant, countless, free,
Then freely, freely give to Him
Who gave His life to set you free.
Oft having little, much they gave,
and in leaner times, still would save
for God's work at home and abroad.
And He, Who always honours His Word
Abundant blessings on them poured
of peace, joy and strength in the Lord.

March on, march on old 'Fuddy-duds',
lift high the cross of Christ your Lord.
No one too old to fight for Him;
None of His Own will be discharged.
Sing to Him, for He calls to you,
* "Let Me hear your voice, so sweet to Me."
Lift then your cracked and shaky voice,
give your Saviour cause to rejoice.
It is the heart song of your love,
which you will sing in Heaven above
clear and sweet, with perfect voice.

References
* verse 1. Psalm 92 14
* verse 2. Psalm 104 16
* verse 3. Job 31 4 — Matt. 10 30
* verse 3. Psalm 90 17
* verse 3. Isa. 46 4
* verse 4. Matt. 10 8
* verse 5. Song of Sol. 2 14

A FATHER'S LOVE

There is a story concerning a tribe of North American Indians, who had a custom that at the age of thirteen, their sons must prove adult status by being left alone all night in a forest.

The time had arrived for a certain boy to go through this ordeal, and at dusk his father took him into the forest and left him there. The boy found his way to a huge tree and flattened himself against it, hoping to go undetected by any prowling animal, if he kept perfectly still. There he remained all night, fighting against drowsiness, and at the least sound pressing harder against the tree.

And then dawn began to break, and he thought he saw a shadow of a man not very far away; trembling, he crouched down hoping to be less discernable. Then daylight began to penetrate into the forest, and, yes, there was a man there! The lad peered anxiously across to see if he might know the man. Yes, he knew him! It was his father! All through the night he had been watching his boy, ready with his bow and arrow in case of any animal approaching him.

What a great story of the love of a father for his child, and it gives us a very faint picture of the love of God for us, for His love is too great for human explanation. So great is His love for us, whose hearts are full of sin, having no love for Him, He gave His only beloved Son to die for us, and through His death on the cross at Calvary, God forgives the sin of all those who acknowledge their sinfulness and accept the Lord Jesus Christ to be their Saviour. As soon as we do this we become a child of God, we experience His loving care for us, and can claim His loving protection at all times, because He is deeply concerned about all that troubles us.

"Like as a father pitieth his children, so the Lord pitieth them that fear Him." *Psalm 103 13.*

HE KEPT THE COMMANDMENT. GOD KEPT HIM

As I write this article there is much discussion going on with regard to Sunday Trading. A heading in a Christian paper reads, "Churches must be ready to give support and advice to members facing a crisis of conscience over Sunday work."

How well I remember a dear man who faced such a crisis many years ago. My husband and I first met him and his wife in 1940 when we went to Essex to help with a Prince of Wales Boys' Camp, where the boys were helping in the war effort by assisting farmers with the harvest. A great change for Cockney lads! Percy was then retired, the children all married and there were a number of grandchildren.

At the time when the crisis arose in the life of Percy and his wife they had a young family of six children, and he worked for a haulage firm, owned by a lady, who one day informed him there was a job to be done which must be done on a Sunday, previously there had been no Sunday work. Percy said he was sorry but he would not work on a Sunday, so he was told if he would not do the job, he was sacked. "Very well," he said, "I shall not work on Sunday, so if you insist, I must be sacked," and he was. Percy, unlike so many people today, knew the commandments and he knew, "Remember the Sabbath day to keep it holy." *Ex. 20 8*. He had always kept it and he always would do so.

When Percy told his wife he had been sacked, she fully agreed with the action he had taken, but what were they to do. Wages were small enough, and here they were with all these little ones to feed and maintain. They did what all who trust their Lord do, they took their problem to Him, knowing He would provide a way for them. And He did. They had little money to spare, but what was available Percy took and went out and purchased a few articles always necessary to people who lived in country villages in those days – candles, matches, tin kettles, oil for lamps and a few other articles. These he put in a box which he strapped to the back of his bicycle and cycled round the villages to sell them.

Percy and his wife were elderly and retired when we had the privilege of meeting them, but he was the owner of two large vans, stocked with a large variety of goods and the business now run by one of the sons. And what a gracious, radiant old couple they were.

Thus was the Scripture fulfilled. "Them that honour Me, I will honour." *1 Sam. 2 30.*

Stand up, be counted for Jesus
  If you love His Name.
'Though others may alter
  Do thou never falter,
Stand up, be counted for Him.

Stand up, be counted for Jesus,
  Stand up straight for Him;
Hide not your head in shame
  Boldly declare His Name.
Stand up, be counted for Him.

Daisy Neal

SUNDAY SCHOOL

How lovely Sundays were when I was a child, and particularly in the summer time, when from azure blue sky the sun shone over our town of Stafford. There were no cars then and the peace and stillness was only broken in the morning and the evening by the ringing of the bells in St Mary's Church.

The Gospel Hall where my parents worshipped was about a mile from our home. I was the eldest of five children, so Mum and Dad took it in turn to attend morning worship, but in the afternoon, when we were able to walk so far, we went with Dad to Sunday School, and when there were only two of us to go with him, we each were able to hold his hand, but when there were three or four of us, we took it in turns.

My father was in charge of the Infants' Class – as it was called in those days – and around forty or fifty little ones attended, ages ranging from three to six. When it was time for school to begin, my father stood in front of the class and waited until all were perfectly quiet, then he lifted his hand in which he held a little pointer, and when he dropped his hand they all said, "Outside Satan, inside Jesus." This was to remind them that they must all behave, and very rarely did any of those little ones misbehave or cause any trouble. They loved my father and he loved all of them.

A dear old gentleman played the little American organ, and when he became too old to make the journey, as I could play well enough by then to take his place, I did so.

All hymns and choruses were learned by heart, and as I write this article I can almost hear them singing, "Do you know what makes us happy, When so many hearts are sad?" And how lustily they sang the chorus, "We are little friends; We are loving friends. We are happy, happy little friends of Jesus." When the children went home, each one was given a little ticket having a picture and a text. When they had six of these they brought them back and were given a larger one, and on returning six large ones, a prize was given to them. How proud they were then!

In the summer the whole of the Sunday School, Infants, Middle Classes and Seniors had an outing on a large field just outside the town, and we took our own mugs. What fun running races and playing games.

And then at Christmas, a party when we had a lovely tea, and afterwards sang and recited and then received prizes for good attendance. Such simple pleasures, but how we all enjoyed these times.

As I look back on these times, I picture again the small room with all the little ones gathered. I can see my father standing before them waiting for perfect silence, and then singing vigorously, as only little children can —

"We are little friends, we are loving friends,
We are happy, happy little friends of Jesus.
We are little friends, we are loving friends,
We are happy all day long."

I should like to think that they all did find happiness in Jesus. I know some of them did.

WHAT! NO TELEVISION!

Almost unbelieveable to most people today, but, nevertheless it is true, I have no television set. Nor did we ever have one when my husband was alive. Perhaps as you read the title to this article and the first lines, you too are surprised and wonder why I have no 'box in the corner'. I will tell you.

When I was a very little girl, even before I was in my 'teens', a very well-known children's evangelist used to come and conduct Missions at our Gospel Hall. His name was R. Hudson-Pope, the man who wrote the chorus, "Cleanse me from my sin, Lord." Do you know it? Through the summer months he also conducted Missions on the sands at seaside resorts, run by the CSSM (Children's Special Service Mission). He was not only a fine children's evangelist but also an accomplished pianist and talented musician. The CSSM chorus books contain many of his works both words and music.

I am grieved that today this chorus book is little used, for the choruses in it are full of Scripture, with wonderful tunes. How can people replace them for so many unscriptural, unpoetical and unmusical ones being sung today! The children. I am afraid are the losers.

Now, on one of his visits to our Gospel Hall, speaking to a gathering of thirty or forty children, R. Hudson-Pope said this; "Don't go anywhere if you would not like Jesus to come with you. Don't say anything you would not like Jesus to hear you say. Don't do anything you would not like Jesus to see you do." These words I have never forgotten.

Some years ago, the Editor of *"This England"* called television, "That Accursed Box in the corner." I firmly believe it is. One day, when the Doctor was visiting my husband, I noticed him looking keenly round the room and I wondered why. Then he said, "How lovely to come into a room where there is no television!" Very interesting remark, I thought.

I once heard a London City Missionary say, "How can you tell little children about the Lord Jesus when they sit up at night with their parents watching, 'Video Nasties'?"

Some years ago, a dear Minister friend of ours, retired after a long ministry which was greatly blessed by the Lord, became so dismayed by the deterioration in TV programmes, he put his set in the back of the car and threw it down the nearest tip!

Right from the beginning of Scripture the Lord has called His people to be a separate people. It is a cardinal doctrine of Scripture. "Come out from among them, and be ye separate," saith the Lord. "Touch not the unclean thing." *2 Cor. 6 17.*

As a result of the teaching I have received since childhood, I should be miserable and uncomfortable if I had 'A box in the corner'. As it is I am happy and contented and the days are not long enough for all I should like to do, and I praise the Lord.

THINK ON THESE THINGS.

SAFE IN THE ARMS OF JESUS

During our years in West Africa, my husband and I had the great privilege of meeting a number of Salvation Army missionaries. What happy memories I have of the loving fellowship we had with them. All extremely hard working; always cheerful; all bearing the likeness of the Lord whom they loved and served.

Of one couple in particular I have very fond memories, for we spent many happy times with them. One particular incident stands out in my memory. We were with them during an Easter period, and at 5 a.m. on Easter Sunday morning we were awakened to the strains of the beautiful Easter hymn, "Christ the Lord is risen today" being played on a concertina. It was Bert welcoming in the day of resurrection. What a wonderful start to the celebration of the great day of our Christian faith.

Elsie came from Manchester, and her family paid little attention to anything connected with Church matters, having much more interest in Variety Shows. When Elsie was a schoolgirl, Madame Patti, the world-famous singer, offered a prize of a course of singing lessons to a Manchester schoolgirl who could be chosen as having the best singing voice. Elsie was the winner. What a beautiful voice she had!

Sometime later, the founder of the Salvation Army, William Booth, held a campaign in Manchester, and Elsie was persuaded by an aunt to go with her to hear him preach, and when she heard the story of Jesus and His love she was overwhelmed when she realised — He loved *her*! She yielded her life to Him, joined the Salvation Army, later becoming an Officer and was posted to London. Now her lovely voice was used in the Lord's service. How very different her life would have been had she not accepted her aunt's invitation to hear William Booth preach.

There in London, in the course of her work, she met Bert, a soldier in the Coldstream Guards, who fell in love with her, but she refused his advances as such a connection would not be allowed for a Salvation Army Officer.

But Bert fell very ill, and Elsie, hearing of this, visited him in hospital and, kneeling beside his bed, prayed that the Lord would heal him and convert him. The Lord marvellously answered her prayer. Later Bert trained as an SA Officer, he married Elsie and after serving in Corps in England they were sent to South Africa, and then to West Africa where it was our pleasure to meet them.

Then retirement came, and as they lived in a flat in Suffolk we often had the joy of meeting them, for we did not live far away. What joy to relive in conversation our experiences together in the tropics.

But Elsie fell ill and a serious operation was necessary. After a few days a Doctor and a Consultant came together to see her, and were pleased to tell her she had done very well, but, imagine their surprise when she said, "Stand up, and bless the Lord!" They said no one had ever said anything like that to them before.

She progressed for awhile, but again became ill and returned to hospital. She was put in a side ward on her own. Her bed was on the opposite side from the door and a little lower down the room. Visiting her one day, Bert quietly opened the door, as he did so, Elsie sat up in bed with a beautiful smile on her face, put up her arms as though greeting someone, and fell back — dead. Bert said, "She was in the arms of Someone else before I could take her into mine."

I am sure, that, as the Lord received His child He said, "Well done, good and faithful servant, enter into the Presence of thy Lord."

TIMELY HELP

For many years, white people who went to tropical regions where malaria was prevalent, took Quinine as a protection against the fever, but when my husband and I went to West Africa, Mepacrine tablets were in use. There were, however, those who still preferred to take Quinine as Mepacrine turned the skin very yellow. Perhaps some of you who read this book will have taken the tablets and know the results.

But to some unfortunate persons this drug was a poison, and I was one of them. Nasty blotches appeared on my face, arms and body; my hair started to fall out and I felt very poorly.

Eventually I was sent to see a Doctor who worked in a large hospital, situated on the coast in the capital city. After an examination he said I must stay in the hospital for a month, in order to receive each week a large injection of an antidote to the poisoning. So, in I went.

By this time my ears were extremely painful. When I mentioned this to the Doctor, he said, "We have a patient here at present with malaria, who is an Ear, Nose and Throat Specialist. I will mention it to him." Next day, this dear man, wearing his dressing gown, came with my doctor to examine my ears. He said he could see nothing wrong with them, but prescribed for Rectified Spirit to be put into my ears every morning. This was done and the result was strange in that a bright yellow liquid came from my ears looking just as though a Mepacrine tablet had been dissolved in water, but gradually the tenderness and pain subsided.

During the last few years my hearing has become dull, and on having my ears examined recently, I was told that there is no doubt that the poisoning of the Mepacrine damaged them. Hearing this I questioned myself, "But, what would have happened if the E.N.T. Specialist had not been in the hospital just when I was there? Possibly it could have meant years of increasing deafness. I have no idea who this man was or where he worked; I only saw him on that one occasion, and I was never able to thank him for what he did for me, and I am so sorry about this.

Only as I have been writing these articles have I realised how many events in my life I have taken as a matter of course, when really they have been interventions by my Heavenly Father on my behalf. Oh! how blind I have been! How ungrateful for His wonderful care for such a thoughtless child. But now, in these days of my "Three score years and ten," *Psalm 90 10,* I have a new outlook, full of adventure; constantly thrilled as I recognise my Father's Hands guiding the daily affairs in my life. Some problems which arise are what some people would call 'trivial', but in the lives of God's children there is nothing too trivial to be outside His observation and His tender care.

"Casting all your care upon Him, for He careth for you." *1 Peter 5 7.*

I SURRENDER ALL

The kitchens of the houses and bungalows in West Africa were always situated at a little distance from the main building, the reason for this being that wood burning stoves were used for cooking. The Garden Boy collected the wood from the forest and brought it to the compound, where he sawed it into suitable lengths which he stacked at the side of the kitchen, in order that the Cook could easily slip out and get logs when he needed them. You can imagine how hot these kitchens were when meals were being prepared. But what wonderful results most of the Cooks produced.

At the time of this story, our Cook was an elderly man who came from Togoland, and a very good cook. Having attended a Presbyterian Church he often sang hymns when working in the kitchen, one of his favourites being, "I surrender all", and his rendering of it was rather unique, for he would sing, "I surrender all," then in a high falsetto, "I surrender a-aal" again. I loved to hear him.

One evening, friends were coming to have dinner with us. The menu had been decided a few days earlier in order to give Cook plenty of time to get everything he needed from market. The day arrived, but in the afternoon there was rather a strange silence around the kitchen, and the Steward and the Garden Boy looked extremely glum, which is so unusual for Africans. At last, they both asked to see me, and hardly knowing what to say conveyed to me the fact that Cook was dead drunk. I asked them what could be done. "No worry, Madame, no worry, we get another cook for you." And they did, for they had already been round to the other bungalows and found a Cook whose Master was going out to dinner and would not need him. We consulted this man and he said it would be quite all right, sent his cook over, and he soon set himself to prepare the meal for us, and it was a lovely one. Africans are very versatile!

Next morning, "I surrender all", sent the Steward up with a parcel. It contained the aprons and other things we supplied for him. He went off and we never saw him again.

How easily and happily he sang, "I surrender all", and it is just as easy for us to do the same, and yet keep back portions for ourselves.

May we all sing from our hearts,

"Love so amazing, so divine,
Shall have my soul, my life, my all."

Oh! help me Lord,
that I may not from Thee withhold
one portion of my heart,
but gladly yield Thee all.
Grant that no sin will dull my ears,
to shut away Thy voice
when Thou dost call.
But ever ready may I be
to do the thing which pleases Thee.

Daisy Neal

LIBERTY

During the years when my husband and I lived in West Africa, the Colony where we were stationed was being stirred up to obtain freedom from British Government to become self-governing. Thus it became a common occurrence, for the rougher type of African, on seeing a white person, to lift up his fist and shout "S.G.".

The Cacao Research Institute where my husband worked, was situated just outside a small village, and as many of the Africans employed at the Institute lived in the village, the white men and their wives were well known to the villagers, and there was a friendly relationship between us.

But, one day, driving slowly through the village, as one had to do, for people walked all over the road, two African men, with a menacing air, came close up to my car, and lifting clenched fists, bawled in my ear, "S.G.". I continued driving slowly, steering with my left hand, and putting my right hand out of the window with my thumb up replied, "O.K.". The two men thought this a wonderful joke, and staggered around the road, holding their stomachs, laughing heartily. But my village friends looked on with amazement at the rude actions of these men toward me. But I know it was the Lord Who prompted me in how to deal with the situation, for had I given 'tit for tat' there could have been trouble.

But the Ghana Church of Pentecost gave their answer to the 'S.G.' adherents in the form of a new chorus —

"I have my liberty,
I have my liberty,
I have my liberty
Now, now, now, now.
My chains are broken down,
Jesus has set me free,
I have my liberty NOW."

How heartily the congregation of this church throughout the country sang this chorus, clapping their hands and swaying to the rhythm — as only Africans can, — gracefully, joyfully, with smiling faces.

What a contrast this chorus to the angry shouts of 'S.G.' by those of the opposite side.

To every person who reads this story, may I ask you, dear Reader, "Which Government have you chosen for yourself? Self Government or the Government of the Lord Jesus Christ Who died, to free from the bondage of sin, all those Who come to Him for forgiveness; for He said, "Whosoever committeth sin is the servant of sin . . . . if the Son — the Lord Jesus Christ — shall make you free, ye shall be free indeed." *John 8 34 & 36.*

Come to Him now and then you, too, will be able to joyfully sing the 'liberty' chorus.